About the
Changing Our World Series

In every generation, there are people who change our world with important contributions in fields such as science, politics, and the arts. These women and men often challenge others' ideas, and have the courage to fight for their own beliefs. Sometimes this fight can mean great personal suffering, or even the loss of their own lives.

Changing Our World books are about some of the people from the twentieth century who have changed the world. Although they are very different from one another, they share one important trait: the determination to succeed. Their accomplishments will last for many generations to come.

Be sure to read all the books in the Changing Our World series:

CHANGING OUR WORLD

BARBARA BUSH

Diane Sansevere-Dreher

A BANTAM SKYLARK BOOK ®
NEW YORK • TORONTO • LONDON • SYDNEY • AUCKLAND

To Ann and John S.

RL 3, 007-011

BARBARA BUSH

A Bantam Skylark Book/September 1991

Skylark Books is a registered trademark of Bantam Books, a division of Bantam Doubleday Dell Publishing Group, Inc. Registered in U.S. Patent and Trademark Office and elsewhere.

Produced by Angel Entertainment, Inc. Cover design by Joseph DePinho

ISBN 0-553-15817-1

Published simultaneously in the United States and Canada

Bantam Books are published by Bantam Books, a division of Bantam Doubleday Dell Publishing Group, Inc. Its trademark, consisting of the words "Bantam Books" and the portrayal of a rooster, is Registered in U.S. Patent and Trademark Office and in other countries. Marca Registrada. Bantam Books, 666 Fifth Avenue, New York, New York 10103.

PRINTED IN THE UNITED STATES OF AMERICA
OPM 0 9 8 7 6 5 4 3 2 1

Contents

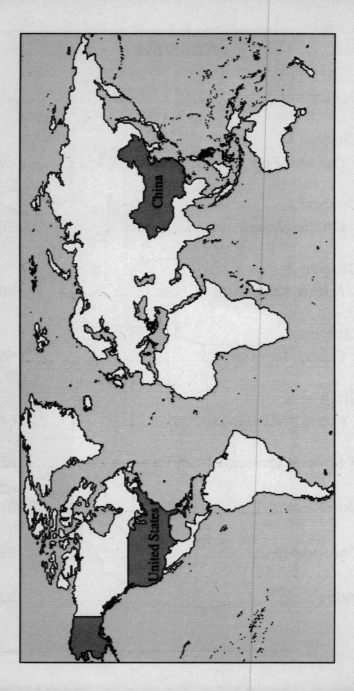

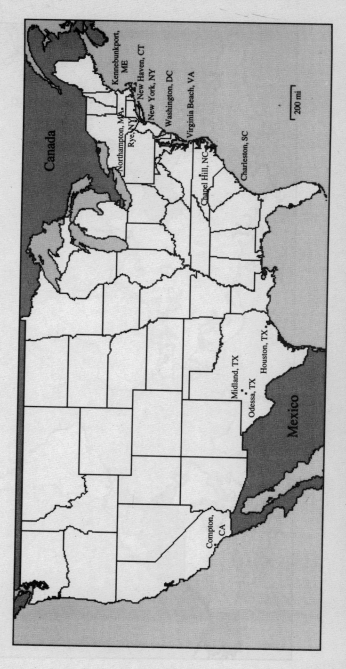

United States Of America

Canada

Mexico

Kennebunkport, ME
New Haven, CT
New York, NY
Washington, DC
Virginia Beach, VA
Northampton, MA
Rye, NY
Chapel Hill, NC
Charleston, SC
Midland, TX
Odessa, TX
Houston, TX
Compton, CA

200 mi

Background

In 1877 Lucy Hayes traveled across the country with her husband, Rutherford B. Hayes, the President of the United States. It was the first time a president had ever gone from the East Coast to the West Coast. Mary Clemer Ames, a reporter covering the trip, called Mrs. Hayes "the first lady of the land." Since then, the wife of the president of the United States has always been called the *first lady*.

The position of the first lady is not an official one. She is not elected by the voters and she does not get paid. But that doesn't mean she doesn't have a job. The first lady has to entertain world leaders, host dinner parties and teas, speak at luncheons, attend special events, and travel constantly. She must answer hundreds of letters every week, run the White House, and supervise her own business staff.

Before 1877 the title of first lady was not used, although presidents' wives still had certain duties.

Even Martha Washington had to give hundreds of dinner parties and teas, and greet all the president's guests in a polite and friendly manner. As the official hostess of the United States, the first lady mainly concerned herself with the running of the White House.

In the 1930s Eleanor Roosevelt changed the traditional role of the first lady. She was a warm and friendly hostess in the White House while her husband, Franklin D. Roosevelt, was president. However, she also moved out of the background by developing a public life of her own.

Eleanor cared about people very much. She was the first lady during the Great Depression, a time when many people lost their jobs and could no longer support themselves or their families. Thousands of people had to stand on breadlines. Eleanor worked in soup kitchens and traveled nationwide visiting poor people on farms and in the cities. The first lady gave lectures, made radio broadcasts, and wrote a daily newspaper column called "My Day." The money she earned was donated to the poor. Eleanor also told her husband, the president, about the poverty and suffering she saw all over the country.

Eleanor Roosevelt was loved by millions of

people. But many others thought the first lady should not be so outspoken. They believed the first lady should stay in the White House. But Eleanor was not content to play hostess and give dinner parties when people all over America were without money and food.

Today it's impossible for the first lady to stay in the background. Reporters often ask her opinions on important political issues. Almost everything she says or does is written in the newspapers or broadcast on television. She is a role model, and she influences the people of this nation.

One way the first lady shows her influence is by her choice of a special project. Every first lady for the past fifty years has adopted a cause. Jacqueline Kennedy, wife of President John F. Kennedy, supported fine arts by helping artists, writers, musicians, and dancers. She had many old works of art in the White House restored. She was also an expert on the history of the White House and even gave tours of the mansion on television, so that the nation could get to know it, too.

Claudia "Lady Bird" Johnson traveled around the country supporting President Johnson's "War on Poverty" and visiting the poor. She chose to join the fight to make America beautiful. She formed committees to direct the cleaning up of wastelands, junkyards, and litter in cities. These committees also supervised the planting of flowers, bushes, and trees on vacant lots.

Pat Nixon redecorated many old rooms in the White House. She restored them to their original beauty. Betty Ford worked at the Hospital for Sick Children, helping the handicapped and orphans. She also promoted the Equal Rights Amendment. Rosalynn Carter helped the mentally ill.

Nancy Reagan took on the problem of drug abuse. In a nationwide campaign Nancy urged young people to "Just Say No" to drugs. Kids all over the country formed "Just Say No" clubs. Today more than five million young students have become involved in the program.

Barbara Bush, our current first lady, has continued this tradition. She has adopted literacy, the ability to read and write, as her special project. Barbara worked for this cause for almost ten years before she became first lady. Her dedicated efforts helped create reading programs in prisons, schools, factories, hospitals, day-care centers, churches, and community centers all over the country.

First Lady Barbara Bush shares a book with children during a Reading is Fundamental book party at the National Zoo. (Rick Reinhard/May 1989)

Being first lady means that Barbara Bush can help even more people learn to read than ever before. She has always loved books, and believes that teaching someone to read is one of the greatest gifts a person can give. She spent hours reading to her own children when they were growing up, and they now read to their children. Barbara says, "Being able to read—whether it's newspapers, magazines, books, even cereal boxes—helps us with day-to-day living and makes life a great adventure!"

Presidents and First Ladies

1789-1797 George and Martha Washington

1797-1801 John and Abigail Adams

1801-1809 Thomas and Martha Jefferson

1809-1817 James and Dorothea "Dolley" Madison

1817-1825 James and Elizabeth Monroe

1825-1829 John Quincy and Louise Adams

1829-1837 Andrew and Rachel Jackson

1837-1841 Martin and Hannah Van Buren

1841 William Henry and Anna Harrison

1841-1845 John Tyler (Letitia Tyler **1841-1842** and Julia Tyler **1844-1845**)

1845-1849 James and Sarah Polk

1849-1850 Zachary and Margaret Taylor

1850-1853 Millard and Abigail Fillmore

1853-1857 Franklin and Jane Pierce

1857-1861 James Buchanan

1861-1865 Abraham and Mary Todd Lincoln

1865-1869 Andrew and Eliza Johnson

1869-1877 Ulysses S. and Julia Grant

1877-1881 Rutherford B. and Lucy Hayes

1881 James and Lucretia Garfield

1881-1885 Chester and Ellen Arthur

1885-1889 Grover and Frances Cleveland

1889-1893 Benjamin and Caroline Harrison

1893-1897 Grover and Frances Cleveland

1897-1901 William and Ida McKinley

1901-1909 Theodore and Edith Roosevelt

1909-1913 William and Helen Taft

1913-1921 Woodrow Wilson (Ellen Wilson
1914 and Edith Wilson
1915-1921)

1921-1923 Warren and Florence Harding

1923-1929 Calvin and Grace Coolidge

1929-1933 Herbert and Grace Hoover

1933-1945 Franklin D. and Eleanor Roosevelt

1945-1953 Harry and Bess Truman

1953-1961 Dwight and Mamie Eisenhower

1961-1963 John F. and Jacqueline Kennedy

1963-1969 Lyndon and Claudia "Lady Bird"
Johnson

1969-1974 Richard and Thelma "Pat" Nixon

1974-1977 Gerald and Elizabeth "Betty" Ford

1977-1980 Jimmy and Rosalynn Carter

1980-1988 Ronald and Anne Frances
"Nancy" Reagan

1988- George and Barbara Bush

1

Bar and Poppy

Barbara Bush would be glad to see that you are reading. Reading has always been a part of her life. Her mother, father, older brother, and even her friend Lucille, who was a year older, read to her before she learned to read by herself.

Every book was a new and exciting adventure for Barbara. She could visit faraway lands and magical kingdoms. She could meet a handsome prince, a wicked queen, or a horse with wings. She could dance all night at an enchanted ball or hunt for treasure in a pirate's cove.

Barbara and her friends, Lucille, Posie, Kate, and June, spent hours acting out scenes from the books they read. They would cut paper dolls out of

Barbara Pierce at age seven in 1932. (Official White House Photograph)

magazines and pretend that the dolls were characters from the stories in the books. Their favorite book was *Little Women* by Louisa May Alcott.

Barbara's parents loved to read. Every evening after dinner and the radio news, her mother and father would each curl up with a book. They encouraged Barbara to learn to read and she grew to love it.

Barbara Bush was born Barbara Pierce on June 8, 1925, to Marvin and Pauline Robinson Pierce. "Bar," as she was nicknamed, was the third child in the Pierce family. She had an older sister, Martha, who was five years old when she was born, and her older brother, James, was three.

Barbara grew up in a suburb called Rye in New York, in a section known as Indian Village. She lived in a three-story house on Onondaga Street with a pond in the backyard. All the houses on her block were large with beautiful lawns and gardens. Most of her neighbors had two cars and a maid. All the people knew each other and the children played together.

Barbara went to the Milton Public School until she was in the sixth grade. After that, she went to the private Rye Country Day School. Every day after school, Barbara played with Lulu, Posie, June, and Kate. They rode their bikes, climbed trees, jumped rope, and floated wax boats down the creek in their neighborhood. In the winter they liked to go sledding. Kate's father tied their sleds to the back of his car and the girls climbed on, swooshing down Stuyvesant Avenue toward the yacht club.

On weekends and in the summer, Barbara and her brother and sister took tennis and swimming lessons at the Manursing Island Club on Long Island. Barbara also took dancing lessons on Friday nights at Miss Covington's Dancing School. There were not many boys in her dance class, so she sometimes danced with other girls. Barbara didn't mind, though. She liked dogs more than boys anyway.

When Barbara was five years old, her brother Scott was born. Two years later, Scott became very sick. He was in and out of hospitals for the next seven years. Barbara's mother spent most of her time with her sick son. Although Barbara missed having her mother around, her father was always there for her and Martha and James. Mr. Pierce did not want any of his children to feel sad because their mother was always at the hospital with Scott. Barbara and her father became very close during this time.

Marvin Pierce was a good athlete. He played baseball and football in college, and he won many trophies for tennis. He loved sports and he passed that love on to all of his children.

A hardworking man, Marvin Pierce also had a good sense of humor. He loved to tease people, as do Barbara and her brothers and sister.

Barbara's mother, Pauline Robinson, had many hobbies. She liked to garden and needlepoint, and she had a great love for animals. She was always caring for injured squirrels and birds with broken wings. She especially loved dogs. When Barbara was seven, her mother's dog had puppies. Mrs. Pierce gave Barbara one of the puppies for her very own. Barbara named the little terrier Sandy. Since then, Barbara has always tried to have a dog in her life.

"All the time our children were growing up we owned dogs," Mrs. Bush wrote in an article for *Life* magazine. "I think they teach children responsibility. And in our busy world it is nice for children to have something warm and furry to hug."

When Barbara was sixteen, she left Rye and started her junior year of high school at Ashley Hall in Charleston, South Carolina. This small, all-girls school was well known because it prepared students for college. The school was also known for turning girls into proper young women. Barbara's older sister,

Martha, had gone there and she left as a mature adult. Mrs. Pierce hoped that Ashley Hall would have the same maturing effect on Barbara.

It took Barbara a long time to get used to school life at Ashley Hall. She had never had to follow so many strict rules. The girls were not allowed to wear makeup. They could not leave the grounds without wearing a hat, gloves, and stockings. The students also could not date the same boy two weeks in a row. Dating meant that a girl would sign up for two seats in the parlor between two and four o'clock on Sunday afternoons. Then she could sit with a boy and twelve other couples in the parlor, along with an adult to watch over them.

Although the school was strict, it did not take Barbara long to make many friends there. Everyone liked her sense of humor. She was best known for her achievements in sports. She held the school record for swimming the longest distance underwater. She also had the record for eating the most hot buttered biscuits in one meal without the headmistress, Miss Mary Vardrine McBee, finding out. She was in the drama club, and had parts in several plays, including Beatrice in Shakespeare's *Much Ado About Nothing* and Viola in *Twelfth Night*.

Life was not all fun and games at Ashley Hall, however. On December 7, 1941 during a drama club rehearsal, Miss McBee rushed into the theater. She announced that the Japanese had bombed U.S. naval ships in Pearl Harbor, Hawaii. The attack forced the United States to declare war on Japan and get involved in World War II.

After the announcement, all the girls hurried to the telephones to call home. Even though the attack had taken place in Hawaii, everyone wanted to make sure that their families were safe. Luckily the holidays were approaching quickly and all the girls would be home with their families soon.

During Christmas vacation, Barbara went to a Christmas dance at the Round Hill Country Club in Greenwich, Connecticut, not far from Rye. She wore a red and green holiday gown and looked cheery and bright as she moved around the dance floor. She was dancing with Jack Wozencraft, a boy she had grown up with in Rye. After the dance was over, a young man asked Jack Wozencraft to introduce him to Barbara. His name was George Bush, and he wanted to know if Barbara would dance with him. She said yes, just as the orchestra started playing a waltz. George didn't know how to waltz, so they sat down and began to talk. They liked talking to each other so much that they talked through several more songs, even though Barbara had come to the dance with another boy! For Barbara and George, it was love at first sight.

The next night Barbara went to the Apawamis Club exchange dance in Rye. George was there, too.

"He literally cut in on me and asked if he and I could have a date," Barbara says. "And my brother [James] cut in on him, which was unforgivable in my eyes . . . ."

James had cut in because he wanted George to play on his basketball team. George joined James' team and offered Barbara a ride home from their first game—it was their first date.

George Herbert Walker Bush was nicknamed Poppy. He grew up in Greenwich, Connecticut, a wealthy town a lot like Rye. Even though Barbara and George lived close to one another, they had never met before. George was seventeen and a senior at Phillips Andover Academy in Andover, Massachusetts. Andover is considered one of the best college preparatory schools in the country. George was home from school for Christmas vacation.

Barbara and George saw each other a few more times during Christmas vacation. After they went back to school, they didn't know when they would see each other again. Charleston and Andover are far apart, but the two teenagers promised to write.

After the Japanese attack on Pearl Harbor, the United States had quickly gotten ready for war. When Barbara returned to Ashley Hall, the dining hall had been turned into a bomb shelter. There were sandbags lining all four walls to support them in case a bomb was dropped near the school. The school had air-raid drills to teach the girls what to do if the city came under attack. It was a frightening time.

At Ashley, Barbara spent a lot of time studying. When she wasn't sitting cross-legged on her bed doing homework, she was knitting socks for George or writing long letters to him.

Barbara and George saw each other only twice the rest of the year. The first time was during spring break and the second was when George invited her to his senior prom.

At George's graduation Henry Stimson, the Secretary of War, spoke. He told the students that even though America needed men to fight in the war, the boys at Phillips Andover Academy could help their country more by going on to college. But George had already made up his mind. He wanted to be a navy pilot. His father had hoped that George would change his mind, but he didn't. On June 12, 1942, George's eighteenth birthday, he went to Boston to enlist in the navy. After that he was immediately sent to pre-flight training in Chapel Hill, North Carolina.

Barbara wanted to help in the war effort, too. She got a summer job at a nuts-and-bolts factory in Port Chester, New York. It was the first job she ever had.

At the end of the summer Barbara went back to Ashley Hall for her senior year. Even though she and George were now living closer to each other, she saw him only once during the entire school year. George was in training and he did not have very much free time. That year he went on to become the youngest pilot in the navy.

In June of 1943 Barbara graduated from Ashley Hall. George invited her up to Maine for two weeks. The Bushes' summer home was on Walker's Point in Kennebunkport. The entire family loved to spend time there. As a small boy George had looked for sea urchins and starfish and gone fishing on his grandfather's boat. For him Walker's Point was a place for family and fun. And it soon meant the same thing to Barbara. She got to know all the Bushes and fell in love with George and with Walker's Point.

Barbara on a vacation trip to Minersing Beach in 1942.
(Official White House Photograph)

George and Barbara became engaged in the fall of 1943. But they didn't have much time to spend with each other. Soon after their engagement, George was called up by the navy. He was sent to fight the enemy in the South Pacific.

Barbara then entered Smith College in North-hampton, Massachusetts. Smith is an all-women's college, but men from nearby Ivy League colleges often visit the campus. During Barbara's first year, though, there were few men around. Most were fighting the war overseas.

Since there was not much dating, Smithies, as the girls were called, went to movies on weekends instead. Barbara kept busy with her friends and as the captain of her soccer team. She did not spend much time on her homework, though. Like many other young women, she could hardly wait for her fiancé to come home from the war.

Meanwhile George was a bomber pilot aboard the aircraft carrier *San Jacinto*. He painted Barbara's name on his Grumman Avenger bomber. George flew missions over Japanese-held islands in the Pacific.

On September 2, 1944 George's plane was shot down during a raid on the island of Chichi Jima, and he was missing in action.

Barbara Pierce and George Bush before their wedding with George's youngest brother, William "Bucky" Bush in 1945. (Official White House Photograph)

At first nobody told Barbara that George was missing. She had left college in the beginning of her sophomore year. She and George had decided to marry on December 19, so she was back in Rye and very busy planning her wedding.

Finally George's parents, Prescott and Dorothy

Bush, told Barbara that their son was missing. But Barbara didn't have to worry for too long. Three or four days later, she heard from George. He said he was all right and that he was coming home!

George returned home on Christmas Eve. After he had been hit, he had turned his plane toward the sea and then jumped out. He had been rescued by an American submarine. He was only twenty years old and had already flown fifty-eight combat missions.

Finally on January 6, 1945 Barbara Pierce and Lieutenant Junior Grade George Bush were married at the First Presbyterian Church in Rye. More than 250 guests attended the reception at the Apawamis Club in Rye. George still felt uncomfortable on the dance floor, but he knew there was no way that he could avoid dancing this time.

Barbara and George spent their honeymoon on Sea Island, Georgia. Then they spent the next nine months moving from one military base to another while George was retrained for combat duty. They lived on bases in Michigan, Maine, and Virginia.

The war in the Pacific seemed endless. Even though she was happy to be married to George, Barbara was constantly worried that his squadron would be called back into action.

Mr. and Mrs. George Bush on their wedding day, January 6, 1945. (Official White House Photograph)

On August 6, 1945 the United States dropped the atomic bomb on Hiroshima, Japan, and the Japanese surrendered. George and Barbara were living in a small apartment near Oceana Naval Air Station in Virginia Beach when President Truman announced the news.

Barbara and George ran outside to join all the people celebrating in the streets. Everyone was shouting, laughing, dancing, and hugging each other. The Bushes slipped through the crowds to their church to thank God for the end of the war.

In September 1945 George entered Yale University to study economics. The Bushes didn't have much money at the time, but neither asked their parents for help. The GI Bill provided money so that the soldiers returning from the war could get an education if they wanted one. George paid for college with money from the GI Bill and part of the five thousand dollars he had earned while he was in the navy. Barbara worked the first year at the Yale Co-op to help pay the bills.

Barbara became pregnant soon after they moved to New Haven, Connecticut and George started at Yale. On July 6, 1946 their first child, George Walker Bush, Junior, was born.

Barbara at Yale in 1945, after George left the navy. (Official White House Photograph)

The Bushes lived in an apartment in a huge old house on Hillhouse Avenue, right next to Charles Seymour, the president of Yale. There were twelve other couples living in the house with them. Eleven of the other couples had one child and one couple even had twins. Altogether there were *forty* people living in the same house.

After George graduated he could have worked for his father in banking or with his uncle on Wall Street. George and Barbara wanted a different kind of life, though. A friend of George's father offered him a job in Odessa, Texas, as an equipment clerk with Ideco, a company that supplies oil drilling equipment. The pay was low, but there was a big future in the oil business for an ambitious young man like George. He and Barbara decided to take the chance.

George graduated from Yale in June 1948. Shortly afterward he headed west in the red 1947 Studebaker that his father had given him when his old car had died. Once George had found a place for the family to live, Barbara and young George followed him to Texas. Even though it was hard leaving all their friends in New Haven, Barbara was excited to start a new chapter in their lives.

2

On the Move

In the late 1940s Odessa was a small prairie town mostly filled with oil drilling equipment. Two movie theaters were the only entertainment in town. The Bushes lived in a small house divided into two apartments separated by a thin wall. They had only three rooms—a bedroom, a kitchen, and another room with a table and chairs. They had to share a bathroom with their neighbors, but they didn't mind. Just having a bathroom was a luxury in Odessa.

George worked very hard for long hours. He was soon promoted to assemblyman and then to salesman. Within a year he was transferred to California as one of Ideco's top salesmen. Barbara and young George went with him as he moved from one big oil strike to the next. George traveled at least a thousand miles a week, driving to the oil fields throughout the rugged California countryside. Barbara was pregnant again and it was hard for her to keep packing and moving. But supporting George was very important to her, so she tried not to complain.

In the middle of October 1949 Barbara's mother and father were in a car accident. Mrs. Pierce was killed instantly, and Mr. Pierce broke several ribs. Barbara wanted to go to the funeral, but her father urged her to stay in California. The baby was due soon and he was afraid the long trip would be too hard. It was very difficult for Barbara to stay, but she knew her father was right.

In December the Bushes' second child was born in Compton, California. They named her Pauline Robinson, after Barbara's mother. She had blond hair and hazel eyes, and everybody called her Robin.

Shortly after Robin was born, George was transferred back to Texas to a town called Midland. There the Bushes bought their first home. It was a small light blue house with its own backyard on East Maple Street. All of the houses on East Maple Street were painted in pastel colors. Everyone in Midland called the neighborhood Easter Egg Row.

The Bushes invited their neighbors over for barbecues and touch football games in the backyard. Since Barbara and George's families lived so far away, they treated their friends in Midland like members of their family instead.

George became restless working at Ideco. He was making money and would surely get promoted, but he wanted more independence. He wanted to be a "wildcatter" and drill for oil. Drilling for oil is a lot more risky, since nobody can tell exactly where the oil is hidden underground. George could lose a lot of money if he dug an oil well and it came up dry. But if he struck oil, he would be rich. George and Barbara decided to take the risk.

With his friend and neighbor, John Overby, George started a new business called Bush-Overby Oil Development. George worked twice as hard and traveled more than ever. All his efforts paid off, though, because his business started to become successful.

Barbara continued to support George in any way that she could. They still did not have enough money for her to go with him on his trips, so she stayed home with the family. She did volunteer work in a nursing home and a hospital. She also helped George start the YMCA in Midland, and raised money for the United Fund and the Little Theater. When George was home they taught Sunday School together.

On February 11, 1953 Barbara gave birth to their third child, John "Jeb" Ellis Bush. George became a partner in another business called Zapata Petroleum. His career in the oil business was now booming. Things could not have been going better for the Bushes.

Suddenly disaster struck. Robin, who was now three, was tired all the time and not eating well. Barbara took her to the doctor and then called George, who rushed home immediately. The doctor explained that Robin had leukemia, a form of cancer. The disease had spread throughout her body and she only had a short time to live. The doctor told them to take Robin home and make her as comfortable as possible.

Barbara and George did everything they could to help their daughter get well. They took her to Memorial Hospital For Cancer and Allied Diseases in New York, (now known as Memorial Sloan-Kettering Cancer Center) where George's uncle was a cancer specialist. Robin was given a new cancer drug. George flew back and forth to Midland for the first few weeks, but Barbara never left Robin's side and she never gave up hope.

Sometimes over the next seven months Robin was well enough to come home to Midland. But she continued to get worse.

Back at the hospital in New York Barbara stayed with Robin day and night. George worked, took care of the boys, and flew up on weekends. Barbara and

---

Leukemia

To understand what leukemia is, you should first know a little about blood. Blood is made up of three things: red cells, white cells, and platelets. Red blood cells carry oxygen through the body. White blood cells fight infection. Platelets are important in clotting the blood and stopping it from flowing when you get hurt. If the body didn't produce enough of these cells, you would be in trouble—fast!

Leukemia is a form of cancer in which the body produces abnormal cells in place of healthy blood cells. People with this disease are often tired and weak, they get sick a lot, and sometimes they have heavy nosebleeds. Leukemia is the leading cause of death by disease for children from two to fifteen. No one knows what causes leukemia, although there are over thirty drugs available to help the body produce normal blood cells again. Still, doctors are a long way from finding a complete cure.

George prayed for Robin as they watched her get weaker and weaker. Barbara asked the doctor why this was happening to her little girl, and he told her something she never forgot: "Every person is a miracle. It takes billions of cells to make up a person. And all it takes is one cell to be bad to destroy a whole person." Since then Barbara has thought of every person around her as a miracle.

When Robin was asleep Barbara would walk the halls of the hospital. She listened to the staff, talked to the other children in the hospital, met their parents, and shared their sorrow. During the entire time that Robin was sick Barbara never cried. She was trying to be strong and cheerful for Robin. But she was feeling the strain. Barbara's hair started to turn gray even though she was only twenty-eight.

In October 1953, just before her fourth birthday, Robin died. Her parents were with her. Barbara finally broke down and cried in George's arms.

Barbara returned to Texas. The loss of Robin had become so painful that she could actually feel the ache in her body.

"I hadn't cried at all while Robin was alive," Barbara said in an interview for *Texas Monthly* years later, "but after she died, I felt I could cry forever."

George remained strong for her. He never left Barbara alone, always making sure that a friend or neighbor was at the house with her.

It was George Junior, only seven when Robin died, who finally shook Barbara out of her grief. One day she heard her son tell a friend, "I can't play today because I have to be with my mother—she's so unhappy." Barbara realized that she had to pull herself together. She knew that she and George were very lucky to have the family that they did.

George's business continued to grow, and so did the Bush family. Neil Mallon Bush was born in 1955. Marvin Pierce Bush was born in 1956 then Dorothy (Doro) Bush in 1959.

During these years George was busy running his company and traveling, so he was rarely home. But his efforts were successful and he began making a lot of money.

For Barbara these years were filled with the family. Since George was away so much, she had to be both mother and father for her five children. She was tough, but she had a soft heart. She was always there for a hug, a word of praise, and plenty of encouragement. And she was also there to tell her children when they were wrong.

Barbara recalled a conversation she once had with her husband when he was away on a business trip: "I called George one day when the boys were small and I said, 'I'm desperate—I don't know what to do. Your son's in trouble again. He just hit a ball through the neighbor's upstairs window.' And George said, 'Wow. What a great hit!' And then he said, 'Did you get the ball back?' "

Barbara was very active in her children's lives. She encouraged each to play sports and join in other activities. Barbara's love for tennis was passed on to all of her children, as was her sense of humor. "We tried to be disrespectful on a regular basis," Marvin Bush once said. "Out of disrespect we called her the Gray Fox."

"We thought her gray hair was funny," added Doro Bush.

Barbara also tried to pass on her love of reading to her children. She read to them when they were very small and had them read to her when they were older. For her son Neil, this was especially important. Neil had dyslexia, a reading disability. His teachers said that he might never go to college because he had so much trouble reading. But Barbara hired tutors for Neil and had him tested. She found books with large print that were easier for Neil to read, and she never gave up. The reward for her hard work came when Neil received both a bachelor's and a master's degree from Tulane University.

In 1959 the Bushes moved to Houston, Texas, the financial center of the oil business. They bought a beautiful home and had enough money for their

---

Dyslexia

Look at these words:

> was
>
> saw

Imagine what it would be like to read a book if you couldn't tell the difference between those two words. Or if the letter "b" looked like the letter "d" to you. Well, that's what reading is like for some people—people who have **dyslexia**.

Dyslexia is a disorder in which people reverse words, letters, and even numbers when they read them. Often they have trouble writing, too. This makes it very hard for dyslexic children to do well in school.

Professionals have not been able to agree on the answer to what causes dyslexia. However, methods of testing and training have been developed that allow many dyslexics to go on to college as other kids do.

---

future and for their children's education. George, now in his mid-thirties, became restless again. He was thinking about new challenges. He was interested in public service and wanted to follow in his father's footsteps and go into politics.

In 1962 George ran for the chairmanship of the Harris County Republican party. Barbara went on the road to campaign with him. When he made a speech, she would sit on the platform and listen. She heard him make the same speech 189 times! George joked that she took up needlepoint during that campaign to keep herself from falling asleep.

Barbara discovered she liked campaigning. She could size up people and situations quickly. She could remember people's names and the things they were interested in. Her abilities helped George from the start of his political career. He won the chairmanship.

Two years later in 1964 George ran for the U.S. Senate. During the campaign Barbara went from door to door, asking voters what they thought of George Bush. She wanted to make sure that she got honest answers, so she didn't tell anyone that he was her husband. Although George and Barbara worked very hard on the campaign, he lost the election.

George then realized that if he wanted to be in

politics, he would have to work at it full-time. He sold his shares in Zapata Oil for one million dollars and became a full-time politician. In 1966 he ran for the U.S. House of Representatives. This time he won. George was the first Republican from Harris County to become a congressman.

The Bushes packed up again and moved to Washington, D.C., for George's new job. Barbara took her children on tours of the city. She wanted them to see and learn as much as they could about

Barbara and George on election night in 1966. George was the first Republican Congressman to get elected to the House of Representatives from Harris County, Texas. (Official White House Photograph)

the nation's capital. Barbara also made many friends in Washington. She would invite friends and neighbors over to the house every Sunday for a barbecue.

Socializing is an important part of a politician's life. Luckily both George and Barbara did this quite naturally since they love being with people. People found Barbara to be smart, warm, and honest. She became friends with many of the congressmen's wives. Barbara also kept busy by welcoming new families to Washington, helping sick friends, and volunteering in hospitals. But her own children always came first. She made a point of being home when they needed her.

Barbara handled the role of a politician's wife easily except when it came to making speeches. As a congressman's wife she often had to lecture to women's clubs. She worked on her speeches long into the night, actually practicing in front of a mirror. Her knees shook—even when she practiced. Barbara was so nervous when she gave a speech that she didn't realize she was a really good speaker. Audiences loved her. Her ideas were very clear and she had a warm sense of humor.

In 1968, the year Richard Nixon was elected president, George was reelected to the House of

Representatives for another two-year term. However, he was already planning to run for the Senate again. Barbara worked hard on George's campaign for the Senate, but he lost the election.

After George's defeat President Nixon chose him to be the U.S. Ambassador to the United Nations. In March 1971 the Bushes moved into the ambassador's residence at the Waldorf Towers in New York City.

Barbara loved it. She had the chance to meet people from the 128 countries in the United Nations and to learn about their cultures.

Barbara was just as proud of her own culture and she decorated their home with paintings by American artists. She served American food and wines at all the receptions and dinners she and George hosted. She took her foreign guests to family picnics in Connecticut and New York Mets home baseball games.

As always Barbara found many places where she could volunteer. One place had special meaning to her. She worked with cancer patients at Memorial Hospital, where she had once spent many months comforting her daughter Robin.

Then the Bushes decided it was time for a new challenge—and that meant yet another move.

3

A New Adventure

In 1974 George Bush went to work for President Ford. Gerald Ford offered George a choice between two jobs—ambassador to London or Paris. Either job would have meant living in a glamorous and exciting city, and socializing with high society. But George and Barbara were not interested in living in a glamorous city. They wanted a new adventure.

George chose the position of American envoy to the People's Republic of China instead. In October of 1974 George and Barbara left for Beijing, China. The only family member who went with them was C. Fred Bush, the dog that Jeb had given his mother for her birthday.

In China the Bushes lived in a walled compound

The Great Wall of China

In China, during the Chou dynasty, many feudal lords built walls along the boundaries of their land to keep their enemies out. More than 2,200 years ago, the first Ch'in emperor connected all of those short walls into one long wall: the Great Wall of China.

The Great Wall of China is about 1,500 miles (2,400 kilometers) long. In some places it is as much as 40 feet (12.2 meters) wide and 50 feet (15.2 meters) high. In others, it may be only 15 feet (4.6 meters) wide and 20 feet (6.1 meters) high. Most of the wall is made of rubble, but some parts are made of hard-packed dirt while some of the passes are made of brick or masonry.

One of the Seven Wonders of the World, the Great Wall is the only man-made creation that can be seen from space.

---

that held all the foreign embassies. Barbara and George enjoyed being together in China. Since the children were still in America, Barbara had the time to really devote herself to George's work. The United States' relationship with China was very important, so the Bushes worked hard to develop trust between the two countries.

Barbara was fascinated by Chinese culture. She studied Chinese, practiced *tai-chi* (an Oriental form of exercise), and learned about Chinese art and history. She often went out to explore the many sights of the country. She visited the Great Wall of China, which is a fifteen-hundred-mile wall built across the northern part of the country. She also visited the ancient Ming tombs where Chinese emperors had been buried hundreds of years ago.

Barbara loved the Chinese people and admired their strong ties to home and family. She and George stopped using the embassy car and rode bicycles, since that was the way most of the Chinese traveled. She was always amazed when she stopped at a streetlight. Before the light turned green, there would be a hundred other bikes lined up next to her. Barbara and George were well-liked and respected by the Chinese.

Their dog C. Fred, however, was not as popular. The Chinese often kill dogs because they roam the streets sick with rabies and steal much needed scraps of food from people. Although there are some dogs in China, there were no buff-colored cocker spaniels like C. Fred. Many Chinese people thought that C. Fred was a cat. Some didn't know what he was and were afraid of him. So Barbara quickly learned to say in Chinese:

"*Ni bu pa. Ta shi shau go. Ta bu yan ren.* Don't be afraid. He's a little dog. He doesn't bite people."

Even though Barbara was happy to have so much time alone with George, she missed her children. During Christmas vacation she went back to the U.S. to be with them.

In the summer of 1975 four of their five children

The entire Bush clan in 1979. Left to right: Top: Marvin, 22; George, 3; Jeb, 26; George; George W., 33; George W.'s wife, Laura. Bottom: Jeb's wife, Columba; Noelle, 2; Dorothy, 20; Barbara; Neil, 24. (Official White House Photograph)

came to China. At that time George Junior was twenty-nine and had just graduated from Harvard Business School. He was planning to enter the oil business in Texas. Neil, twenty, was an undergraduate at Tulane University, and Marvin, nineteen, was getting ready to enter the University of Virginia. Doro was about to celebrate her sixteenth birthday. Twenty-two-year-old Jeb and his wife, Columba, had to stay in Houston, where Jeb was working at the Texas Commerce Bank.

During the children's visit to China, the Bushes planned to have Doro baptized. China is a communist

---

The Bush Family

President and Mrs. Bush have five children and twelve grandchildren. Mrs. Bush is very proud of all her children and believes they have grown up to be wonderful people.

This is who they are:

George Walker Bush, Jr., is a businessman in Dallas, Texas. Mrs. Bush predicts he will make a great governor of Texas one day. Jeb is a realtor in Miami, Florida. Neil is in the oil and gas business in Denver, Colorado, and Marvin is a partner in an investment firm in Virginia. The Bushes' only daughter, Dorothy, works in public relations in Washington, D.C.

country where religion is not encouraged and they had a difficult time even finding a church. The Bushes were finally able to locate a Christian church in Beijing for the ceremony.

Barbara loved living in China, but she was thrilled in December 1975 when the Bushes returned to Washington, D.C. George had been given a new job as the director of the Central Intelligence Agency (the CIA).

Even though Barbara was glad to be back in the United States, she was not too happy about George's new job. She and George had always spent long hours talking about George's work. As the head of the CIA, George now had to keep America's secrets from leaking out to foreign countries and was not allowed to discuss his job with Barbara. The Bushes had also spent a lot of time socializing with friends before George took over at the CIA. Now George could no longer be directly involved in politics, and the Bushes could not even attend any political social events.

It was a difficult time for Barbara. She had felt important and alive in China because she had been so actively involved in trying to improve U.S. relations with China. Now there were no political campaigns to get excited about. All the children were grown-up.

The Central Intelligence Agency

The Central Intelligence Agency (CIA) was established in 1947 to provide for the security of the United States by gathering and reporting facts from abroad. The Federal Bureau of Investigation (FBI) is the other security service in the United States. But the FBI investigates violations of Federal law and threats to the internal security of the United States. The CIA investigates threats to national security from other countries.

By reading foreign newspapers, magazines, and books, watching television and listening to radio broadcasts from other countries, and by traveling around the world, CIA employees look for information that is important to the safety of the United States. Since most of what they do is kept secret, nobody even knows how many people work for the CIA.

Besides gathering information, CIA agents also advise foreign leaders. But they have been criticized for taking a too active role in the internal affairs of other countries and getting involved in military matters.

She had no role in George's work and no important projects to call her own. Even though Barbara continued to do volunteer work in a nursing home, entertain guests, and speak at luncheons, her life still felt empty.

After a year as director of the CIA, George wanted to get back into politics. In November 1976 Jimmy Carter, a Democrat, was elected president. George Bush resigned from the CIA and he and Barbara returned to private life. They moved to a new home in Texas and took some time to travel around the world. When they were home, Barbara was often with her grandchildren.

By the summer of 1978 George was sure that Jimmy Carter would not be reelected. He decided to run for president himself. He invited experts from the Republican party to Kennebunkport to help him plan his campaign. When Barbara wasn't busy finding places for their guests to sleep and preparing food for them, she sat in on their strategy sessions.

After the meetings Barbara would jog by herself and think about all the issues she had heard in the meetings. She realized that many things bothered her about her country—the growing number of homeless people, people addicted to drugs and alcohol, and teenagers dropping out of school. She thought about how to reduce crime and unemployment, and how to work for world peace.

George announced that he was running for president on May 1, 1979. Barbara knew she was more

---

RIF
Reading Is Fundamental

RIF gets kids to read! As America's oldest and largest program to prevent illiteracy, RIF organizes special activities for children, holds workshops for parents, and gives away free books to young people.

All of the work is done by volunteers in the local communities. Thanks to Mrs. Bush's support, RIF now has more than 111,000 volunteers.

There are 11,000 sites where RIF programs are at work —schools, libraries, community centers, Head Start programs, housing projects, migrant worker camps, Native American reservations, homeless shelters, and wherever there are children who need to learn how to read. To date, RIF has helped more than 2.4 million children and given away more than 100 million books!

---

than ready to take on the challenge. If George won the election and became president, she would be expected to take up a special cause. Barbara had a long history of doing volunteer work. With George as president, she'd be able to help even more people as first lady.

Barbara set out to find her project. She learned there were many people who could not read or write well enough to get through day-to-day life. Many young people dropped out of school because they had learning disabilities. Adults often could not get jobs because they could not read the ads in the "help-wanted" section of the newspaper or fill out job application forms. Barbara saw that when some of these people couldn't get jobs, they turned to crime and ended up in prison. Many were on welfare or became addicted to drugs and alcohol.

Barbara decided that, as first lady, her main project would be to work on literacy. She would help more people learn how to read and write well enough to lead full and positive lives.

Barbara soon had a chance to work for literacy. The president of Reading Is Fundamental (RIF), a nationwide program that encourages children to read, asked Mrs. Bush to be a board member. Barbara quickly accepted the position. This was her big start.

George got off to a big start as well. He did very well in the early primary elections. Primaries are held by the Republican and Democratic parties in each state. Often several Republicans or Democrats want to run. It is the job of the people voting in the primaries to choose just one person to represent each party in the national election.

George won the most votes in all of the primaries except New Hampshire, and had a big victory in Iowa. By January 1980 he was the front-runner for the Republican party.

George's lead did not last long, however. Ronald Reagan began to win the primaries in other states. He soon won enough votes to make him the Republican candidate for president.

On May 27, 1980 George withdrew from the race. He and Barbara were both disappointed, but they promised to help the Republican candidate get elected.

Several months later the Bushes went to the Republican National Convention in Detroit. When they got to their hotel suite, the telephone rang. It was Ronald Reagan. He asked George to be the vice-presidential candidate on the Republican ticket. George accepted. Barbara ran over and hugged George, knowing that Ronald Reagan and George Bush would be a hard team for Jimmy Carter and his running mate, Walter Mondale, to beat.

And they were. On the night of the national election, George, Barbara, and their family watched as the Reagan-Bush ticket won a very convincing victory over Carter-Mondale.

4

Going National

On Inauguration Day January 20, 1981, Ronald Reagan and George Bush were sworn in as the President and Vice President of the United States. That evening the Bushes attended many parties and celebrated with 150 of their relatives.

Once again they moved into a new home—the Vice President's House. The Vice President's House is a big, old Victorian home that sits on ten acres of land. It has a helicopter pad, a tennis court, and wonderful views of the Capitol, the Washington Monument, and the Naval Observatory.

Barbara had an office on the third floor. She kept her exercise bike and running machine there so she could sneak in a little exercise whenever possible.

Almost immediately Barbara went to work on her project to promote literacy. She proved that even a "second lady" could help the cause. She found out that twenty-three million adults in our country were unable to read and write beyond the fourth-grade level. About thirty million had developed their skills to only an eighth-grade level.

Barbara realized that she had a lot of work ahead

Barbara feels that reading aloud to kids is the best way to instill a love of books in them. Here, she reads to some youngsters during a Reading Is Fundamental book event at Sterling Elementary School in November 1983. (Rick Reinhard/Reading Is Fundamental)

of her, but she was ready to work hard. She knew how important it is that as many adults as possible become literate. Children whose parents cannot read or write are unlikely to be able to read or write themselves.

In her eight years as second lady, Mrs. Bush attended 537 events related to literacy. She made people aware of the problem. She encouraged them to volunteer to teach others how to read and write. She told them that literacy is "being able to read and write and doing it well enough to help you live your life." Barbara gave speeches, appeared on television and radio, visited schools, hospitals, prisons, and anywhere she could to encourage people to read.

In 1983 she wrote a book, *C. Fred's Story*, about the adventures of their cocker spaniel's life in China. She gave the money she made from the sale of the book to two organizations that help people to learn to read.

In December 1985 the American Broadcasting Company (ABC) and the Public Broadcasting Company (PBS) began a nationwide campaign called "Project Literacy U.S." (PLUS). This was a big breakthrough for Barbara and her cause. PLUS created TV shows about the problem of illiteracy that were shown on both ABC and PBS. They developed stories about literacy for some of the TV series. Many people became more aware of the problems facing those who can't read or write. Barbara is given much of the credit for the success of PLUS.

The work that Barbara Bush loved most was meeting new readers in the many programs started by her literacy campaign. She visited a prison where inmates had been trained to teach other prisoners to read and write. A young man stood up and read a letter that he had written to her. Mrs. Bush's eyes were filled with tears when he told her how ashamed he had always been of not being able to read and write. He said that now, as a literate person, he knew he would be able to live a better life.

There was another man whose courage Mrs. Bush admired. J.T. Pace was sixty-three years old and had just learned to read. He appeared with Mrs. Bush before a live TV audience of 800,000 people for the ABC Fourth of July Special promoting literacy. J.T. was going to read the Preamble to the Constitution. Just before the show started, J.T. got scared. There were still some long words that he had a hard time pronouncing and he did not want to read on stage. Barbara told him that sometimes she had a hard time with long words, too. She explained that many readers have the same problem, and said to him, "What if you and I read the Preamble together?"

J.T. thought about the idea for a moment and then smiled. "I'd like that," he said.

Barbara and J.T. stood on the stage and began to read the Preamble together. J.T. stumbled a bit in the beginning, but soon he became confident and began reading in a strong, clear voice. Barbara's voice faded off. J.T. finished reading all by himself!

Besides helping adults combat illiteracy, Barbara is also concerned with children's reading problems. She has worked very hard to help children experience the joy of reading. Since 1981 she has been involved in RIF, which has given away almost one hundred million books to children.

In addition to her special projects, Barbara had other responsibilities as the vice president's wife, especially as a hostess. She entertained heads of foreign countries and their wives, ambassadors, astronauts, princes and princesses, athletes, and movie stars at over two thousand gatherings. Traveling all over the world with George, Barbara visited all fifty states as well as sixty-eight foreign countries.

As busy as she was, Barbara still found time to have friends over for dinner, a movie and popcorn, or

Barbara greets Raisa Gorbachev at a reception in Washington, D.C., in 1987. (David Valdez/The White House)

a barbecue and horseshoes. She also continued to do all kinds of volunteer work, including visits to shelters for the homeless. Barbara often put on an apron and served food in soup kitchens all over Washington.

By 1987 the Bushes had lived in the vice president's mansion for seven years. It was the longest time they had spent in one house.

However, George was ready for a new challenge by this time—and a new address. He decided to run for president again in the 1988 elections. Barbara and the rest of the Bush family geared up for another national campaign. Because George had maintained a fairly low profile while serving under Ronald Reagan for two terms, Barbara wanted to show people the real George Bush—the warm and loving father and husband she loves and respects.

She traveled from state to state with a slide show of scenes from their life. There were pictures of George at the Great Wall of China, at the Berlin Wall, and with world leaders. Finally there was a slide of the whole family, including their new dog, Millie, sitting in front of their Kennebunkport home. Barbara ended her speech saying, "Here we are, the whole Bush family, dedicated to electing this man for president."

Barbara went to almost every state in the country during the campaign. During her travels another national problem came to her attention. In practically every city she visited, Barbara saw growing numbers of homeless people. She tried to help them in any way that she could. When she stayed in hotels she took unused soap from her room to give to the homeless. She told her staff to do the same.

This was the beginning of Operation Soap. She asked her staff and reporters on the Bush campaign to save unused soap and the small bottles of shampoo to distribute at women's shelters. One hotel that found out about Operation Soap did not put *any* soap in her room when she arrived there. Another, however, thought Operation Soap was such a good idea that the hotel also began to give soap to homeless shelters.

During this time Barbara was closely watched by the press. Television and newspaper reporters said and wrote many positive things about her projects. But some made fun of her gray hair, her wrinkles, and her figure. She was criticized for not wearing makeup or fashionable clothes. Some joked that she looked so much older than George that she could be his mother.

Barbara brushed off the comments, saying, "What you see is what you get." She cared more about whether someone had a place to sleep, or food to eat, or knew how to read, than about her wrinkles, hair, weight, and clothes.

Some people criticized her for being old-fashioned and for not having a career of her own. One television interviewer said to her, "Your husband is a man of the 1980s. You're a woman of the 1940s. What do you say to that?"

Barbara calmly replied that being a wife and mother of five children was her career. It was the choice she had made, and Barbara had never regretted it.

Despite the time Barbara spent on the road campaigning with George, she continued to support many of her literacy projects.

In May 1988 she took her twin granddaughters to the National Zoo in Washington, D.C. to the hatching of the "Readasaurus" egg. A Readasaurus is a make-believe dinosaur that has supposedly been living since the beginning of time because it learned to read. The Readasaurus egg hatched and out popped Rex and Rita Readasaurus. They asked children to send them postcards listing three books they had read during the summer. By the end of the summer, more than *one million* children had sent postcards to Rex and Rita at the National Zoo.

Finally the primary elections were over. George Bush had won a convincing victory over the other Republican candidates, but he wouldn't be officially named their nominee until the Republican National Convention beginning on August 15.

After the hectic months of campaigning, the Bushes were happy to get away to Kennebunkport to relax for a few days before the convention began.

George Bush was named the official Republican

In May 1988 Barbara took her granddaughters, Barbara and Jenna, to the "hatching" of Readasaurus twins. (Rick Reinhard/Reading Is Fundamental)

candidate for president during the convention in New Orleans, Louisiana. He chose Dan Quayle, a senator from Indiana, as his running mate. George Bush and Dan Quayle would run against Michael Dukakis, the governor of Massachusetts, and his running mate, Lloyd Bentsen, a senator from Texas.

Barbara knew it would take a lot of work to ensure a Republican victory in the presidential elections and she worked tirelessly to make the move to the White House. She eagerly traveled across the country

Before the Republican National Convention, the Bushes relaxed together in Kennebunkport. Here, Barbara catches up on her gardening. (David Valdez/The White House, August 1988)

giving speeches and interviews, visiting schools and nursing homes, day-care centers and hospitals, and shelters for the homeless. She covered as many as twenty cities in twelve states in one week's time.

Barbara enjoys cooking for the Bush clan in Maine as they wait anxiously for the Republican convention. (David Valdez/The White House, August 1988)

Whenever she was back at the vice president's house, there was no time to relax. Hundreds of letters were waiting to be answered and what little time she had with nothing to do was spent baby-sitting her grandchildren.

The people of the United States were able to keep up with Barbara's hectic pace throughout the campaign. She kept a diary of her travels, which appeared weekly in *USA Today*. Besides detailing her packed schedule, she wrote about the wonderful programs around the country that taught people to

Barbara and George arrive at the Republican Convention in style—under the president's seal. (David Valdez/The White House, August 1988)

read and others that helped the poor, the hungry, and the sick.

During the last week of campaigning the pace picked up even more. Finally time ran out. There was nothing left for Barbara and George to do except wait for the results.

Barbara and George with his running mate, Senator Dan Quayle, his wife Marilyn, and their three children in August 1988. (David Valdez/The White House)

5

In the White House

On election night November 8, 1988, George Bush won the election over Michael Dukakis, the Democratic candidate. Later that night George and Barbara, with their family next to them, stood before a cheering crowd of supporters. The race was finally over, but their work had just begun.

Before George was to be sworn in as president, the Salute to the First Lady was held at the Kennedy Center, honoring Barbara. At that ceremony she displayed her sense of humor by joking with all the reporters who had said she had dressed like a frump during the campaign. She stood up in front of the audience, opening her jacket to show off her blouse and said, "Please notice—hairdo, makeup, designer

Barbara and George walk to their new home at 1600 Pennsylvania Avenue followed by the cheers of the crowd lining the roads. (David Valdez/The White House, 1989)

dress. Look at me good this week, because it's the only week."

On January 20, 1989 Barbara stood outside the Capitol with George. She held two bibles—the Bush family bible and the one used by the first American President, George Washington, two hundred years

Inauguration night was almost more hectic for Barbara and George than the campaign had been. They had to go from ball to ball to thank all their supporters. (Michael Sargent/The White House, 1989)

earlier. As millions watched the inauguration on TV, George Herbert Walker Bush was sworn in as the forty-first president of the United States and Barbara Bush became the country's first lady.

That afternoon Barbara and George rode at the head of the parade toward the White House. Then they got out of the limousine and walked along the street, waving to the 300,000 people holding American flags who lined the road. The Yale band played George's old school song. Cameras clicked everywhere as the first couple took their first steps to their new home at 1600 Pennsylvania Avenue.

George and Barbara arrived at the White House and found all their belongings already unpacked. Everything had been put in its place in the drawers and closets. For the first time after twenty-nine moves in forty-four years of marriage, Barbara didn't have to unpack a thing! The household staff had wanted to surprise them.

After all the celebrating was over, it was time to get down to business. George got right to work at his desk in the Oval Office. And Barbara assumed the role of the first lady, which she called "the most demanding volunteer job in the country!"

Perhaps the biggest change was adjusting to

The White House

There are 132 rooms in the White House. On the first floor of the Main Building, many rooms are open to the public. The kitchen, the library, and the office of the White House doctor are also on the first floor.

The public is never allowed on the second floor where the president lives. There are three bedrooms, some dressing rooms, a sitting room, a kitchen, and a family dining room in the West Wing off to the side of the Main Building.

Extra bedrooms for guests, a pool room, a sun room, and staff quarters are on the third floor. The White House also has a bowling alley, swimming pool, and even a movie theater!

The East Wing is where most of the White House staff works. The president's Oval Office, though, is separate. It is in the West Wing.

living in the White House. Barbara was used to the privacy of the vice president's house. There she could take long walks, let the dog out in her bathrobe, and tend to her flowers any time she wanted.

In the White House, because the family quarters are located above the president's offices, there are always many staff people and Secret Service agents around. The first lady can't even wear her bathrobe through most rooms of the house, and she can only take short walks on the lawn around the driveway. She also has to keep the dog out of the flower beds. However, there are some advantages to living in the White House. There are many guest bedrooms so there's always room for friends and family to stay over.

In the first three months the Bushes hosted nearly one hundred events. They included formal dinners, "Friday Night at the Movies," and hot dogs and horseshoes on the South Lawn. And then in March, to top it all off, the family dog, Millie, gave birth to six puppies!

Barbara begins each day by taking Millie for a walk and then either plays tennis or swims. After that she gives interviews to the press and reads her mail. She answers letters, writes speeches and articles, and attends luncheons, coffees, and teas with special groups of people. She may have a coffee and cake party with several adults who have just learned to read. Or she might meet with school principals to give them a pat on the back for their good work.

Once she gave a big party on the White House lawn for the RIF "Reading Is Fun Week" and invited two hundred children. There were circus clowns,

Barbara, Millie, and her six puppies take in some sun on the White House lawn in March 1989. (Carol T. Powers/The White House)

storybook characters to greet the kids, and musicians to entertain them. They also got to meet Millie's six new puppies. Millie seemed happy to show them off to the children.

Even after a full day of work, Barbara's day is not yet over. She attends state dinners or receptions with

Every day Barbara must answer stacks of mail and write many letters no matter what else she has to do. Luckily she's got a computer to help her out. (Carol T. Powers/The White House, 1990)

the president. Sometimes she hosts dinners at the White House for ambassadors, senators, or other public officials. Every night before going to bed, the first lady writes even more letters, prepares speeches and anything else she needs for the next day, and tries to make time to pick up her latest book and read a little.

Since Barbara has become the first lady, she has demonstrated concern for more national problems. She spends many hours trying to make the public more aware of the plight of the homeless, AIDS patients, the poor, as well as those who have never learned to read.

For many years on Thanksgiving and Christmas, Barbara has quietly slipped into the Ronald McDonald House in Washington, D.C. which provides shelter for families of children who have serious illnesses. She has always brought cakes and cookies to cheer up the families. In 1989 she invited the press to come along on one of her visits. She spoke with children, their families and staff members, and posed for pictures with them for the press. After her visit, photographs of Barbara at the Ronald McDonald House appeared in newspapers and magazines all across the country.

Barbara took George and some reporters to the Children's Inn at the National Institute of Health in Maryland. The Children's Inn is a new facility for families of children with life-threatening diseases, much like the Ronald McDonald House.

It may seem as if Barbara likes to have reporters follow her all over the country and put her picture in papers everywhere. But she invites the press with her to make the public more aware of the hardships these children and their families face. She also hopes to encourage other people to help them.

Another recent national problem Barbara is very concerned with is AIDS. AIDS is a life-threatening disease that strikes both children and adults. Many AIDS patients are cared for in special shelters. Unfortunately, there are many AIDS patients who are not well cared for at all because family members and some health care workers are afraid of catching the disease. Barbara has visited many of these shelters to give comfort to the patients.

Of all the projects Barbara is involved in, promoting literacy is still the most important to her. In her efforts to get more people to learn how to read and write, she began the Barbara Bush Foundation for Family Literacy. The foundation encourages nation-

Barbara often asks photographers to take pictures of her holding children with AIDS. She hopes to show the public that hugs and care do not spread the disease. (Carol T. Powers/The White House)

wide efforts to involve parents in literacy programs. Barbara believes that parents are their children's first and best teachers because she thinks that literacy is passed from generation to generation.

Since it started in March 1989 the BBFFL has given over five hundred thousand dollars to literacy programs across the country. The money came from donations made by companies and individuals who care about literacy.

Barbara even got her dog, Millie, to donate to her project. *Millie's Book*, as dictated to Barbara Bush, is the story of Millie's life in the White House. It was published in the fall of 1990 and has been on the *New York Times* bestseller list for a long time. Millie agreed

---

Millie: "The First Dog"

The Bushes' dog, Millie, is called the first dog. In March, 1989, Millie gave birth to six puppies: five boys and one girl.

Millie has an exciting life at the White House. The first lady walks her and feeds her at six A.M. At seven A.M. she usually goes to the Oval Office to check up on the president. Once in a while she goes on press interviews with Mrs. Bush. In the afternoons Millie chases squirrels on the White House lawn. In the evening before going to bed, she sometimes drops in on a White House party to greet guests. After a long day the first dog retires to the president and Mrs. Bush's bedroom where she has her own bed.

No matter how involved Barbara may get with other causes, she will always have enough time to read aloud to children. Literacy remains her special project and number-one priority. (Carol T. Powers/The White House, 1989)

to donate all the money made from the sale of the book to the BBFFL.

Barbara wants every child to share in the joy of reading and listening to a wonderful story. To reach as many children as possible, Mrs. Bush hosted a Sunday evening radio show called "Mrs. Bush's Story Time" from September through November 1990. Joined by her friends Mickey Mouse, Big Bird, Bugs Bunny, and other characters, she read aloud favorite book selections to children all over the country.

Since becoming the first lady, Barbara has visited Poland, Hungary, the Netherlands, South Korea, Japan, and China. While the president meets with world leaders, Barbara visits hospitals, schools,

Even though Barbara loves visiting other countries, she and George are always happy to come home to their children, grandchildren—and dogs! (Susan Biddle/The White House, 1990)

and homes to see how other nations try to solve the same problems we have in our country.

Barbara is also eager to show our foreign visitors the wonderful programs at work in this country to help the poor, sick, and homeless. She and George have welcomed many world leaders, foreign dignitaries, and members of royalty to the United States.

In March 1989 Barbara was diagnosed as having Graves' Disease, a thyroid gland disorder which causes weight loss, swollen eyes, and double vision. After many months of medication and radiation therapy, Barbara was cured. Through her own fight with Graves' Disease, Barbara has been able to teach the public more about it. Barbara didn't take much time off because nothing seems to stop her from doing the things she enjoys, and supporting the causes and people who are important to her.

The most important person in Barbara's life is her husband, George. As president, everything he says and does is watched closely by the public. Sometimes the public does not approve of his actions. Barbara is quick to support him at these times, especially when she believes the criticism is unfair.

During the summer of 1990 many people questioned the way that President Bush handled the crisis in the Persian Gulf. In early August Iraq's Saddam Hussein ordered his troops to invade Kuwait. In an article in *People* magazine, Barbara explained the situation to her grandchildren by saying, ". . . a perfectly peaceful country was sitting there and another country invaded it, and that we cannot have."

The United States and other countries of the United Nations placed an embargo on Iraq and Kuwait. This meant that no food or anything else was allowed to go into or come out of either country.

Several nations, including America, sent troops, artillery, tanks, and planes to Saudi Arabia, a country which borders Iraq and Kuwait. They also sent naval ships to the Persian Gulf, hoping that the presence of a large military force would pressure Iraq to withdraw its troops from Kuwait.

During this time President Bush went on vacation with Barbara and the family for three weeks at their home in Maine. No matter what was going on, the Bushes have always spent the month of August in Maine.

That summer, however, many Americans were upset with the president for going on vacation while U.S. soldiers were being sent into possible danger in the Persian Gulf. Many people thought the president should have stayed in Washington, D.C. to handle the crisis.

Barbara felt the criticism of George was unfair. In an interview with *People* magazine, she said, "You

Even though the public felt the president shouldn't be vacationing in August 1990, when American lives were on the line in the Persian Gulf, Barbara felt Maine was the best place for George to get a handle on the situation. (David Valdez/The White House)

know, you're not away in this job. No matter where you are." She explained that many of George's aides came to Maine, as did Jordan's King Hussein and Saudi Arabia's Prince Saud. Barbara knew that Maine was a good place for George to concentrate on the situation in Kuwait.

Barbara and George were both worried about the U.S. soldiers being sent to the Persian Gulf. In her interview in *People* magazine, Barbara said, "I hate it because families are being broken up. I feel just like any other mother would. How do you think George feels—that's what kills me—because he really feels each one of those [sons and daughters] are his."

Barbara has also been criticized. There are some people who think she is not a good role model for American women.

In the spring of 1990 Barbara was asked to be the guest speaker at the graduation ceremony at Wellesley College, an all-women's college in Massachusetts. A quarter of the seniors graduating signed a petition against her appearance at the ceremony because they believed that Barbara is a woman who has become known because of her husband's achievements and not her own. These women graduates had been taught to strive to become the president of the United States, not the president's wife.

Barbara was not offended by her young critics because she does not disagree with them. She knows she is best known as President Bush's wife. Today many young women would be unhappy with that title. But Barbara has chosen to remain in the background supporting George, and she likes it that way.

When the students at Wellesley listened to her speak during their graduation ceremony, they discovered that Barbara Bush had some important things to say. She told them, "At the end of your life, you will never regret not having passed one more test, not winning one more verdict, or not closing one more deal. You will regret time not spent with a husband, a friend, a child, or a parent."

She advised, "If you have children they must come first. Your success as a family, our success as a society, depends not on what happens at the White House, but on what happens inside your house."

The women students began to clap and cheer as she concluded, "And who knows? Somewhere out in this audience may even be someone who will one day follow in my footsteps, and preside over the White House as the president's spouse. I wish him well!"

The next day even her critics agreed that Barbara Bush had given the speech of her life!

The support she gives to her husband, her loyalty to family and friends, and her strength to do what she believes in despite public pressure, have made Barbara Bush one of the most popular first ladies of modern times. Many people look up to her as a role model.

It is clear Mrs. Bush enjoys her role. She once said, "I love my life. I consider myself to be the luckiest woman in the world!"

"The luckiest woman in the world!" (Carol T. Powers/The White House, 1989)

A Special Message from Barbara Bush

Barbara Bush has spent many hours giving encouragement to those who cannot read. However, she has much more work ahead of her. There are still many people who need and want to learn how to read and write. Everyone can help Mrs. Bush on her special project, even you. Her special message, published in a New Jersey newspaper, will tell you how.

First you can be good readers yourself. Turn off the TV once in a while and put down that Nintendo game and pick up a good book, newspaper, or magazine. You won't be able to put it down once you get started.

In school, pay attention when the teacher is teaching you how to spell, how to use good grammar, how to read and write. These are the lessons that will help you all your life.

If some of your classmates are having a tough time, don't be afraid to help them. And never, never make fun of them. Next time it might be you who needs help.

And please, don't forget your little brothers and sisters. Okay, maybe they are a bother sometimes, but if you take the time to share a storybook with them, maybe they won't be such a pain, and you will be giving them a gift that will last all their lives—good reading habits.

Quick Facts

United States

- **Capital City** = Washington, D.C.
- **Date of Independence** = July 4, 1776
- **Government** = Democracy
- **Head of Government** = President George Bush
- **Area** = 3,618,770 square miles
- **Population** = 247,498,000
- **Population Density** = 68 per square mile
- **Life Expectancy** = male 71.5 years; female 78.5 years
- **Population Age** = 21.5% under the age of 14
- **Adult Literacy** = 99%
- **Per Capita Income** = $16,444
- **Currency** = Dollar
- **Chief Crops** = corn, wheat, soybeans
- **Chief Industries** = service, manufacturing, finance

Chronology

1925   Barbara Pierce is born on June 8.

1941   The Japanese attack Pearl Harbor on December 7.
Barbara meets George Bush during Christmas vacation.

1942   George turns eighteen on June 12 and enlists in the U.S. Navy.

1943   Barbara graduates from Ashley Hall in June. She and George become engaged in the fall, and Barbara enters Smith College when George is sent to the South Pacific.

1945   Barbara and George marry on January 6.
The United States drops the atomic bomb on Hiroshima on August 6.
George enters Yale in September.

1946   George Walker Bush, Jr., is born on July 6.

1948   The Bush family moves to Texas.

1949   Pauline "Robin" Robinson Bush is born in December.

1953   John "Jeb" Ellis Bush is born on February 11. Robin dies of leukemia in October.

1955   Neil Mallon Bush is born.

1956   Marvin Pierce Bush is born.

1959   Dorothy "Doro" Bush is born. The Bush family moves to Houston, Texas.

1962   George runs for Chairmanship of the Harris County Republican Party and wins.

1964   George runs for U.S. Senate and loses.

1966   George runs for U.S. House of Representatives and wins. The family moves to Washington, D.C.

1968   Richard Nixon is elected president. George is reelected to the House of Representatives.

1971   George is named U.S. Ambassador to the United Nations in March. Barbara moves her family to New York City.

1974   George is named American envoy to the People's Republic of China.

1975   George is named director of the CIA. He and Barbara move back to the United States in December.

1976   Jimmy Carter is elected president in November. George resigns from the CIA.

1979   George announces he's running for president on May 1.

1980   George withdraws from the race on May 27. Republican presidential nominee, Ronald Reagan, asks George to be his running mate in July.

1980   In November, Ronald Reagan and George are elected as President and Vice Predent of the United States.

1981   President Reagan and Vice President Bush are inaugurated on January 20.

1983   Barbara writes *C. Fred's Story*.

1984   President Reagan and Vice President Bush are reelected in November.

1985   Project Literacy U.S. (PLUS) campaign begins in December.

1987   George decides to run for president.

1988   George is nominated for president by the Republican Party at the National Convention in New Orleans, Louisiana, on August 15.
George is nominated for president by the Republican Party at the National Convention in New Orleans, Louisiana, on August 15.
In November George Bush and Dan Quayle are elected as President and Vice President of the United States.

1989   President Bush and Vice President Quayle are inaugurated on January 20.

In April the Barbara Bush Foundation for Family Literacy is created. Barbara is diagnosed with Graves' Disease.

1990   In August Iraq invades Kuwait. U.S. troops are deployed in the Persian Gulf.

Barbara writes *Millie's Book* in the fall.

1991   U.S. and allied troops attack Iraq through planned military air strikes on January 16.

Index

About the Author

Diane Sansevere-Dreher received her B.A. in Communications from New York University. She has worked in public relations and as a marketing consultant in the book, audio, and video industries. She has published numerous articles in magazines, including *Billboard*, *Sight and Sound Marketing*, and *Software News*. This is her second book for children.